·GROWING UP IN·
Ancient Egypt
ROSALIE DAVID

Illustrated by
ANGUS McBRIDE

EAGLE
BOOKS

Published by Eagle Books
A division of Quarto Publishing plc
The Old Brewery
6 Blundell Street
London N7 9BH
England

A CIP catalogue record for this
book is available from the British
Library.

ISBN: 1-85511-059-8

Design by James Marks
Edited by Kate Woodhouse

Printed in Singapore
by Star Standard Industries (Pte) Ltd.

Contents

Introduction 4
Who were the ancient Egyptians? 6
Cities, towns and villages 8
The countryside 10
The boy-king Tutankhamun 12
The house 14
Daily life 16
Pets and toys 18
Early education 20
At the market 22
Dinner time 24
Visiting the doctor 26
Getting married 28
Fact file 30
Index 32

Introduction

Egypt, in north Africa, has one of the world's oldest civilizations. Its northern shores lie on the Mediterranean Sea. To the west is the Western Desert and to the east is the Red Sea. But the most important waterway in Egypt is the River Nile.

The Nile flows from the south into a fan-shaped delta where it meets the Mediterranean. Egypt has very little rainfall, and without the Nile the entire country would be a desert. Before modern dams were built to hold the water back, the river would flood every year, bringing down thick, black mud from the mountains of central Africa and spreading it over the river banks. This fertile mud enabled the early Egyptians to grow plentiful crops. The ancient Egyptians named their country *Kemet*, which meant "black land", because this was the colour of the rich soil. The land beyond was called *Deshret*, or "red land".

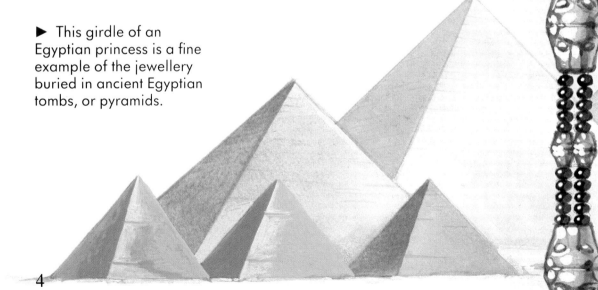

▶ This girdle of an Egyptian princess is a fine example of the jewellery buried in ancient Egyptian tombs, or pyramids.

4

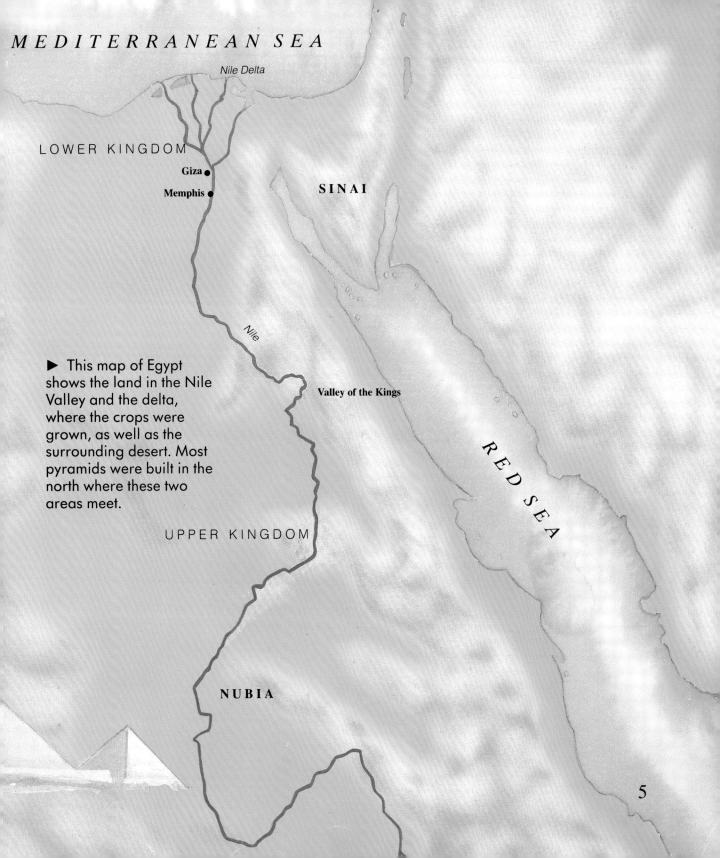

MEDITERRANEAN SEA

Nile Delta

LOWER KINGDOM

Giza ●

Memphis ●

SINAI

Nile

Valley of the Kings

R E D   S E A

▶ This map of Egypt
shows the land in the Nile
Valley and the delta,
where the crops were
grown, as well as the
surrounding desert. Most
pyramids were built in the
north where these two
areas meet.

UPPER KINGDOM

N U B I A

5

Who were the ancient Egyptians?

People have lived in Egypt for thousands of years. About 6,000 years ago, people in the Nile Valley began to develop the way of life we call ancient Egyptian. They began to build large, mud-brick tombs for their rulers, to make beautiful objects for their tombs and homes, and to use a kind of writing. People from Mesopotamia may have settled in Egypt at this time, but no one is sure about this.

▼ The king drove into battle in his chariot, pulled by a pair of horses. He was armed with a bow and a quiver of arrows. Horses were introduced into Egypt in about 1550 B.C. Since they were small, these horses were used only to draw chariots and not for riding.

Two kingdoms gradually developed, one in the north called the "red land" and another in the south known as the "white land". Each had its own king, who wore a special crown. About 5,000 years ago, the king of the south conquered the north, and Egypt was united. The king's name was Menes, and he founded Egypt's first capital at Memphis. There were no more wars for hundreds of years.

Cities, towns and villages

If you visit Egypt today, you can stand with one foot on rich cultivated land and the other in the desert. Thousands of years ago, the cultivated land was kept for growing food and raising animals. People used the desert to bury their dead. The poor people dug shallow graves and covered them with a mound of dirt and stones. The rich people built stone tombs. Stone was also used to build temples. Many of these stone buildings still survive.

Most villages stood along the banks of the Nile. The towns, which were often quite large, were important market centres or special places where gods were worshipped.

Building a royal tomb or pyramid was a major task, so the king sometimes decided that the workers and their families should be housed in a new town. Many children grew up beside the pyramids, and helped with the building as they grew older.

▼ These houses were built on the east bank of the Nile. The houses had flat roofs where people slept in summer.

8

▼ The pyramids and tombs were on the west bank. The Egyptians believed the Land of the Dead was in the west.

9

The countryside

The Egyptians made as much use as possible of the rich soil provided by the Nile mud. They devised a system of irrigation to distribute the water. The *shaduf* was a pulley and bucket that took the water from one level to another. The people grew cereals, vegetables and fruit, and kept animals for food and leather. They kept cows, sheep, goats, pigs and poultry. They also hunted wild animals on the edges of the desert.

Flax was grown to make linen for clothes, and the papyrus plant gave them writing paper, ropes, boats, sandals and baskets.

Most people worked on the land. They grew enough to feed themselves and people who did not work on the land. There was a taxation system, but as money was not used until about 525 B.C., people paid in food and goods.

▶ Peasants worked in the fields, growing crops and looking after their animals. On the right is a *shaduf*, used to bring water from a channel up to the land.

10

The boy-king Tutankhamun

The king of ancient Egypt was called a *pharaoh*. This name comes from the word "peraa", which meant the great house or palace where he lived. The Egyptians believed that the pharaoh was half-god and half-human and was therefore able to ask the gods for their blessing for himself and for all Egyptians. They believed the pharaoh was very important to Egypt's security and prosperity.

Today, Tutankhamun is the most famous of Egypt's kings because his is the only royal tomb in the Valley of the Kings that has been discovered almost untouched. It was found by the archaeologist Howard Carter in 1922 after many years of digging. The king's tomb contained his preserved body, called a *mummy*, a gold head mask and three golden coffins, as well as clothing, jewellery, perfume, furniture and games. The Egyptians believed that the dead needed their possessions to use in the next life.

► Tutankhamun met with his ministers at the royal court. He wore a double crown to show that he was ruler of Upper (south) and Lower (north) Egypt, and he carried the king's symbols of power, the crook and the flail (whip).

The house

Both rich and poor people built their houses of mud-brick and wood. Mud-brick was ideal building material in a hot country with little rainfall. In long-established cities and towns where space was limited, houses with two or more floors were built close together. In the new towns, wealthy people built single-level villas surrounded by gardens full of flowers and trees with a lake or pond.

Even the smaller houses often had four rooms with an outside courtyard. The women cooked in pottery ovens built in the courtyard. Inside, the walls were plastered and painted with scenes of animals and the countryside. There were stools, chairs, low tables, beds and boxes to hold clothes, make-up, jewellery and household items. Some houses had oil lamps, and windows with no glass.

Ordinary Egyptians prayed at home to gods such as Bes, a jolly dwarf-god, and his wife Tauert, the hippopotamus goddess. People kept statues of some of the gods in their houses.

▼ In this house, the columns were carved in the shape of plants. The windows had no glass, but slats let light into the rooms. The house was the centre of many activities such as cooking, eating, sewing and entertaining.

14

Daily life

Small children lived with their mother and other female relatives in a special part of the house. The children's clothes were simple and made of linen. Sometimes they had leather or reed sandals, and most wore a bracelet or necklace of beads. It was the custom to shave boys' heads, leaving only one plaited lock. This was cut off when the child reached 12 years.

When their sons were four years old, fathers began to train them in their own profession or trade. Most girls married and looked after the house and their children.

The Egyptians loved their children, but sadly many died at birth or when they were small. Their parents tried to prevent accidents and illness by spells and charms. Many paintings and statues show children as important people in the family group.

▶ Children enjoyed helping in the house and around the village. The weather was hot, so they spent much of the daytime outside. Here, a mother grinds corn to make bread. Her son holds a cat, the family's favourite pet.

Pets and toys

Most Egyptian families had pets. These animals can be found in many of the painted wall-scenes in tombs. The cat was a favourite pet because it killed rats and mice in the house, and the Egyptians believed that the cat-goddess, Bast, protected the home. Some cats may have been specially trained to help their masters when they hunted birds.

▶ Most families had pet cats, ducks or geese. Rich people kept special dogs for hunting. Egyptian children played with many different kinds of toys. They had balls, tops and pretty dolls with real hair fixed into holes drilled into the head. Some children took part in acrobatics or wrestling competitions.

18

Children had a variety of toys and games. Some of these toys were buried in children's graves so they could play with them in the next world. Other toys have been found in the remains of houses. There were dolls, balls, tops, animal toys and a board game rather like draughts. Some children made their own toys, but there were also toy-makers.

Early education

Between the ages of 4 and 14, boys and girls attended school together, where they learned to read, write and do mathematics. Those who were going to become doctors, lawyers or scribes studied the sacred writing called *hieroglyphs*. They had to copy out stories and religious writings. Some of these exercises survive today. The children also played games, wrestled and learned to swim.

When boys were 14, they followed their father's trade or profession, which could be working in the fields or joining the craftsmen in government or temple workshops. They could also go on to become doctors, scribes, lawyers or government officials. Girls usually stayed at home with their mother to learn how to look after the house.

▶ As the teacher read a story to the class, the children copied it on to pieces of broken pottery or flakes of limestone. Paper, made from papyrus, was too expensive for school work. The children wrote with reed pens and red or black ink.

21

At the market

Each town held a market where people bought food, clothing and household goods. People needed only simple clothes in such a hot, dry country, but they wore jewellery made of pottery or stone, or sometimes gold, silver or copper. Rich people covered their heads, as protection against the sun, with wigs made of real hair or grass.

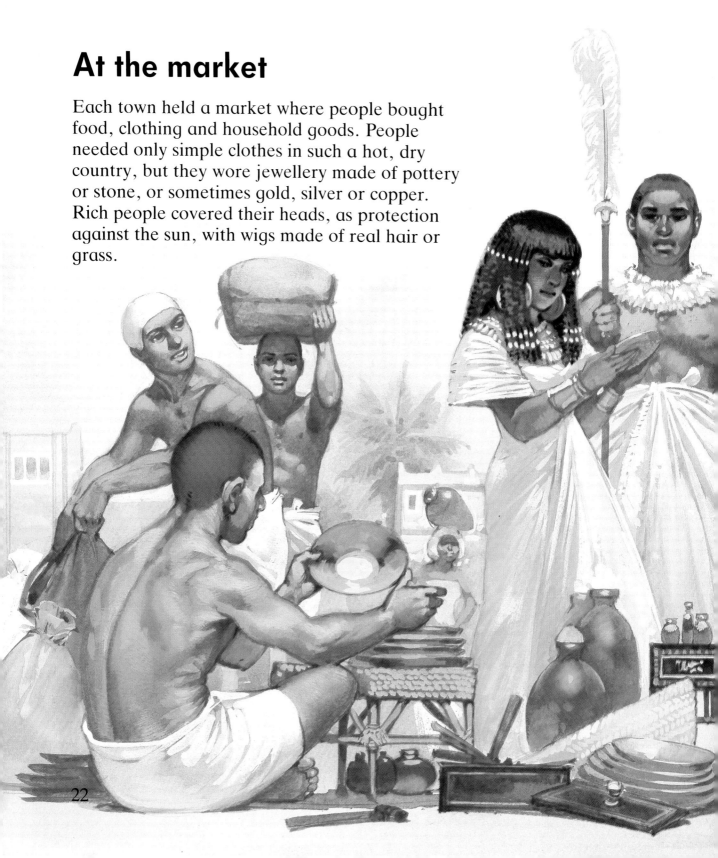

▼ Fruit, vegetables, animals, clothing, pottery vases and dishes were exchanged at the market, which was held outdoors. Many people brought the food they had grown or the goods they had made, to sell by barter.

Pottery cooking pots and serving dishes were for sale, as well as wooden furniture inlaid with ebony and ivory, or beautiful boxes for make-up.

Egyptians had a lot of gold but not much wood, so they imported cedar wood from Syria. Other goods such as silver, ostrich feathers, ebony and ivory came from Asia Minor, the Aegean islands and Nubia, part of present-day Sudan.

Dinner time

The rich soil from the Nile's flooding meant that farmers could grow plenty of cereals, vegetables and fruit. They grew barley, emmer, which was a kind of wheat, lentils, cucumbers, beans, leeks and onions, as well as dates, figs and grapes. Beef was the Egyptians' favourite meat, but they also ate lamb, pork, goat, fish, duck and goose.

The basic foods for poorer people were bread, onions and other vegetables and fruit. Rich people enjoyed much greater variety, including cakes sweetened with honey.

▼ Wealthier people had servants who helped them in the house. Ancient Egyptians did not use knives, forks or spoons. They ate meat and poultry with their hands, and dipped bread into the other dishes.

Food was cooked in clay ovens in the courtyard and served in pottery dishes at low tables. At midday, some women took a meal to their husbands in the fields and to their children at school.

Priests in the temples served three daily meals to the gods' statues so the gods would help the Egyptians. The food was later removed and divided among priests as payment for their duties.

25

Visiting the doctor

Many Egyptians became ill from diseases caused by sand and water. Sand in the air caused lung disease and breathing difficulties, and sand in bread wore down people's teeth. Diseases carried by worms in river water caused many problems. The Egyptians also suffered from many other illnesses we have today.

The Egyptians probably had the world's earliest medical profession. There were doctors and nurses, and medical students were trained at the temples. Doctors performed operations and created medicines. Some medicines were unpleasant, to frighten away the evil spirit that was thought to cause the illness. Many treatments were recorded in ancient medical documents, with practical remedies as well as magical spells. There was even an attempted cure for the common cold.

▶ Here, a doctor attends to a boy's injured knee. An assistant reads out the ingredients and instructions for making a medicine, while another attendant prepares the treatment.

Childbirth was dangerous, and many mothers and babies died. There were special magical spells designed to protect the newborn and their mothers.

Today, scientists gather information about the ancient Egyptians' diseases, diet and lifestyle by examining their mummies. They x-ray the mummies, study their blood groups and examine their body tissue under a microscope.

Getting married

People in ancient Egypt married young. The boys were usually 15 and the girls were about 12. Most people died in their forties, so their lives were short.

Young people chose their partner and wrote love songs to one another. The earliest love songs in the world come from Egypt. Although marriages were not arranged, parents and friends tried to ensure that boys and girls from similar homes and backgrounds met one another.

Egypt today is a very different country. But many of the earlier writings and drawings have been preserved, so we have an excellent idea of what it was like to grow up in such an ancient civilization.

▼ A newly-married couple moved their furniture and other possessions into their new home. Neighbours made the couple welcome, with good wishes for a happy marriage.

▼ There were laws protecting marriage property. The house, furniture and other goods were owned by both husband and wife. A man could divorce his wife, but she kept any valuable possessions she brought to the marriage, and her husband had to make payments to her.

Fact file

The gods

There were state gods (in control of the whole country and the king's protectors) and local gods (each powerful in a specific town or area). These gods had temples and priests who were their "servants". There were also priestesses who sang and danced in the temples. Ordinary people prayed to household gods in their own homes.

Mummification

After death, the bodies of rich people were mummified. The major body organs (except the heart and kidneys) were removed and the body and organs dried, using natron (a natural mixture of salts). The embalmers wrapped the mummy in layers of linen bandages. They placed special jewellery between the layers, to bring the person good luck in the life after death. The preparation of the mummy lasted for 70 days, and then the family buried the body in a tomb.

Embalmers mummifying a body.

Mummification preserved the body so that the dead person's soul (Ka) could recognize it when the Ka returned to the tomb. The Egyptians believed that the Ka then entered the mummy for a short time, so the dead person could eat the food that his relatives had brought to the tomb.

The pyramids

In some periods, the kings built pyramids as their tombs. These were perhaps intended to look like the sun's rays and to provide a ramp for the dead king to join his father, the sun-god. Near the pyramids at Giza, a "sun boat" was found and excavated. The Egyptians may have believed that the dead king used this boat to sail across the sky. Peasants, who were not slaves, built the pyramids.

The end of Egyptian civilization

Ancient Egyptian civilization lasted for about 5,000 years, but towards the end the country was overcome and ruled by foreigners. First came the Assyrians and the Persians, followed by Alexander the Great in 332 B.C. When he died, the country passed to his general, Ptolemy. The Ptolemies then ruled Egypt, ending with Queen Cleopatra VII. The Roman general Octavian finally took Egypt in 30 B.C. and it became a province of the Roman Empire.

Writing

Egyptian language was written in three scripts: hieroglyphs (usually used for texts about history or religious beliefs), hieratic and demotic (both used for business and everyday matters because they were easier to write). Hieroglyphs were a form of picture-writing with over 700 signs. In 1824, a Frenchman, Jean François Champollion, worked out how they should be read, using the Rosetta stone (now in the British Museum). This stone had an inscription written in Greek, hieroglyphs and demotic, honouring King Ptolemy V.

HIEROGLYPHIC					HIERATIC			DEMOTIC
2700 – 2600 B.C.	2500 – 2400 B.C.	2000 – 1800 B.C.	C. 1500 B.C.	500 – 100 B.C.	C. 1900 B.C.	C. 1300 B.C.	C. 200 B.C.	400 – 100 B.C.

Index

animals 7, 10, 16, 18
armour 7
Assyrians 31

barter 10, 23
Bast 18
Bes 14
bread 16, 24, 25
burials 8, 12, 30

Carter, Howard 12
cats 16, 18
Champollion, Jean François 31
chariot 7
charms 16
childbirth 27
children 8, 16, 18, 19, 20, 28
Cleopatra 31
clothes 10, 16, 22
cooking 14, 25
courtyard 14
crops 4, 10, 24
crown 7, 12

dead, burial of 8, 12
demotic script 31
desert 8
Deshret 4
diseases 26
divorce 29
doctors 26
dogs 18
double crown 12

eating 25
education 20
embalmers 30

farmers/farming 4, 8, 10, 24
flax 10
flooding 4
food 8, 10, 24, 25, 31
furniture 14, 23, 28

games 18, 19
Giza 31
goddesses 14, 18
gods 8, 12, 14, 25, 30, 31,
graves 8, 19

hieratic script 31
hieroglyphs 20, 31
history of Egypt 4, 6, 31
horses 7
houses 8, 14
hunting animals 18

illnesses 26
imported goods 23
irrigation 10

jewellery 4, 12, 16, 22, 30,

Ka 31
Kemet 4
kingdoms 7
kings 7, 8, 12, 31

lamps 14
Land of the Dead 9
linen 16
love songs 28

markets 8, 22, 23
marriage 28
medicines 26
Memphis 7
Menes, King 7
Mesopotamia 6
mud-bricks 6, 14
mummies 12, 27, 30, 31
mummification 30, 31

natron 30
Nile River 4, 8
Nile Valley 6

ovens 14, 25

paper 10, 20
papyrus 10, 20
parents 16
peasants 10, 31
Persians 31
pets 16, 18
pharaoh 12
picture-writing 31
priestesses 30
priests 25, 30
Ptolemy 31
pyramids 4, 5, 8, 9, 31

Roman Empire 31
Rosetta stone 31

school 20
servants 25
shaduf 10
soul 31
spells 16, 26, 27,
sports 18, 20
stone 8
sun god 31

taxation 10
temples 8, 25, 26, 30
tombs 6, 8, 9, 12, 18, 30, 31
towns 8
toys 18, 19
Tutankhamun 12

Valley of the Kings 5, 12
villa 14
villages 8

wigs 22
women 14, 16, 25
wood 14, 23
writing 6, 10, 20, 31

Contents

What are homes?   6

Settlements   8

Locality   10

Designing buildings   12

Home materials   14

Inside   16

Big homes   18

Small homes   20

Mobile homes   22

Eco-homes   24

Unusual homes   26

Glossary   28

Index   30

Words that appear in **bold** can be found in the glossary on pages 28–29.

What are homes?

Homes are where we live. Around the world you can see homes of different shapes and sizes. The first homes were very simple with one room and a fire for cooking and keeping warm.

People around the world live in very different homes – from large brick buildings to small mud huts.

Cities and villages

Our homes can be found in cities, towns or villages. In the city, many homes are crowded together in rows of houses or blocks of **flats**. In villages, homes usually have more space around them.

Inside and outside

The inside and outside of a home can look different from place to place. The design of a home will depend on where you live, what the weather is like and what the local building **traditions** are.

This traditional Moroccan home has wooden shutters and painted tiles. They decorate the home and keep it cool.

Home detectives

Homes can tell us a lot about a place. Old buildings are usually made of **materials** that were found locally long ago. Large houses built with expensive materials are the homes of rich people. Homes that are crowded together often show an area where lots of workers live.

This large house is the home of a rich family. It was built with expensive materials and is in beautiful surroundings.

Settlements

Long ago, people chose a place to build a **settlement** carefully. A hill was good for defence against attack, a valley provided **shelter** from the weather and a **fertile plain** was good for growing crops.

By the water

Big cities, such as London, New York and Sydney, grew from settlements built around the mouth of a great river. Ships brought in people and **trade** from overseas. The river carried people and goods inland.

New York City grew when people travelled to the USA by boat to begin a new life.

Growing settlements

Settlements grow bigger over time. Towns and cities usually begin as a few houses clustered together. Over the years, newer houses are built around the edges as more people move to the area. In contrast, in a modern **new town**, the homes are all built within a few years of each other.

Old and newer houses stand next to each other in a city that has been growing for hundreds of years.

Find out the history of your area

1 With an adult, take photos or draw sketches of the different styles of homes near to where you live.

2 Can you find out when they were built?

3 Which is the oldest home you can find? Which is the newest?

How old is your home?

My house - 1999

A new block of flats

Oldest house - 1820

9

Locality

Your **locality** is the area where you live. It might be the countryside, the seaside, a busy city or a housing estate. Going for a walk around your neighbourhood will tell you about your locality.

City or suburbs

In the city, many people live in flats. They don't have a car, so they walk or take the train or bus to work. **Suburbs** are the areas around the edges of a city. People who live in the suburbs often have further to travel to work or to the shops.

A suburban house usually has a garage. The family may use the car to drive to work, school or the shops.

In a village

Homes in the centre of a village can be very old. They have often been there for hundreds of years. Newer homes are built around the edges of a village.

This village in France was built around an old church.

Find out about your locality

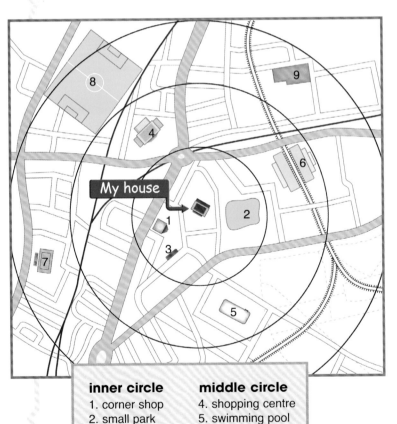

My house

inner circle
1. corner shop
2. small park
3. bus stop

middle circle
4. shopping centre
5. swimming pool
6. train station

outer circle
7. petrol station
8. playing field
9. school

1 Print a copy of a map of where you live from the Internet with your home in the centre of the map.

2 Mark your home. Draw a small circle with your home in the centre.

3 Now draw two more circles each larger than the one before.

Write a list of everything that you can see within each circle.

Designing buildings

Homes around the world have many different designs. They are often built with local materials and designed to suit the landscape and **climate** of an area.

Shelter

Homes are built to shelter us from the weather. Where there is lots of rain and snow, homes have sloping roofs. In areas that flood, houses are built on stilts to keep them above the water. In hot countries, thick walls and small windows keep out the heat.

This house in Thailand has stilts to keep it above the water.

Traditional Japanese houses have wooden frames and paper walls.

Earthquakes

Homes built in earthquake zones, such as Japan, are in danger of falling down during an earthquake. They are designed and built to move, but not collapse, if the ground shakes.

12

Match the homes

You will need:

- card • scissors
- pencils and pens

1 Draw your own pictures of these children and homes onto playing-card sized rectangles.

I live in a hot, dry place

3 Take it in turns to pick a card. Turn the card over to show your friends. Then pick another card. Have you matched a child with their home? If yes, take the cards. If not, replace them. The winner is the person with the most 'matched' cards.

I live where we have earthquakes

2 Shuffle the cards and put them face down on the floor.

4 Add to the game by finding some more children and their homes.

I live where it often floods

I live in a cold, snowy place

Home materials

Homes all over the world are made from lots of different materials – from reeds and mud to concrete and steel. What is your home made from?

Local materials

People traditionally used to build their homes from materials found nearby. Local rock makes a strong, long-lasting material. Trees provide wood for log cabins in forests and reeds are used to build homes near a lake.

In Scotland, old houses called crofts have walls of stone and roofs made with turf. The materials were taken from the rocky fields where these houses were built.

Modern materials

Modern homes are built from **manufactured** materials, such as concrete, glass, metal and plastic. These strong, long-lasting materials are often cheap to make and can be easily transported to different areas.

This tall, strong building is made from steel and glass. It has good views from the big windows.

Do a survey of the materials used to build your home

Make a chart like the one below to record the materials used to build your home both inside and outside.

	Glass	Metal	Brick	Wood	Tiles	Plaster	Plastic	Concrete
Windows	✓			✓			✓	
Doors	✓			✓				
Walls			✓			✓		
Pipes		✓					✓	
Roof					✓			
Floors				✓	✓			✓

Inside

Homes keep us safe and give us shelter. A home is somewhere to spend time and to sleep. Homes are also a place to store our belongings.

Different rooms

Inside our homes, we divide the space into rooms or areas for the different things we do. Bedrooms are for sleeping, the kitchen for cooking, the bathroom for washing and the living room for relaxing.

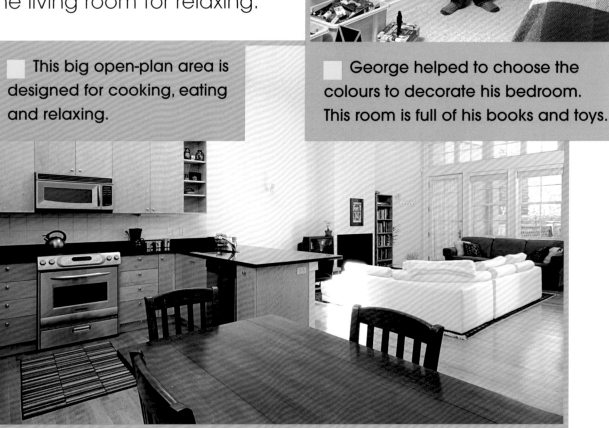

This big open-plan area is designed for cooking, eating and relaxing.

George helped to choose the colours to decorate his bedroom. This room is full of his books and toys.

Floor plan

A floor plan is a drawing that clearly shows the layout of the inside of a home. It is an **aerial view** looking down on the rooms from above. It gives important information about the size and number of rooms.

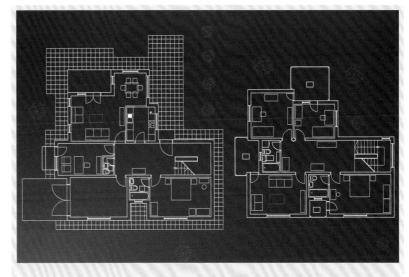

This is a floor plan of a house with two floors.

Design a house

1 Draw a floor plan of a house you would like to live in.

2 Think about who will live with you. What will you all need? How many floors will there be? How many rooms? Will there be a garden?

3 First, draw the ground floor. Any floors you add will need to fit on top. You can choose the number and size of the rooms on each floor.

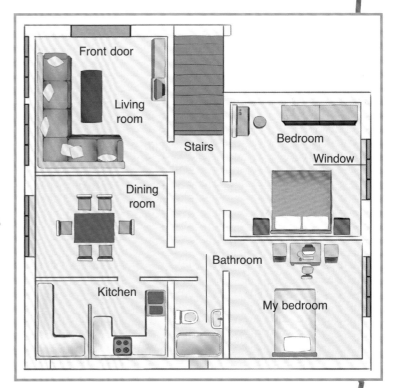

Big homes

Sometimes, rulers and rich people build palaces, villas and mansions to show off their power and wealth. These huge houses are built with expensive materials, such as marble, and are protected by high walls.

Tourist attractions

Some grand historic homes are open for you to visit. You can look at these impressive buildings, learn about their history, see paintings and other treasures and enjoy the beautiful gardens.

The people of the USA built the White House as a home for their president.

Fairytale castle

About 150 years ago, King Ludwig II of Bavaria (in Germany) built Neuschwanstein Castle for his home. Walt Disney modelled Sleeping Beauty's palace on the outline that Neuschwanstein Castle makes against the sky.

Neuschwanstein Castle was built high on a hill.

Make a silhouette of a house on a hill

You will need:
- paper – black and blue
- pencil • scissors • glue

1 On the black paper, copy in pencil the shape of the castle in the picture above (or use your imagination to draw your own castle, palace or mansion).

2 Cut out the shape of your building and the shape of a hill.

3 Stick the shapes onto the blue paper to make a silhouette of a house on a hill.

Small homes

Small homes can be useful in areas where there is not much space. Because land and buildings are very expensive, small homes are also cheaper to buy.

Industry and farms

Small cottages on farmland were traditionally homes for farm workers. In towns and cities, rows of small houses were built quickly and cheaply for workers in factories, mills and mines.

These houses were built close together. Each house shares side walls with its neighbours.

One room

In some of the poorest parts of the world, large families live together and sleep, eat and cook in just one room. After a war or a natural disaster, such as an earthquake, survivors live in crowded temporary camps or shelters.

This African boy is cooking over a fire. The room is also his family's bedroom.

Make a model one-room house

You will need:
- 2 card circles the same size (draw around a side plate)
- scissors • brown and yellow paint • self-hardening clay
- art straws • glue

1 Fold one circle into quarters and cut out a segment. Fold the circle round and glue the sides together to make a cone for the roof. Cut a hole at the top for the chimney.

2 Paint the other circle brown. Draw a smaller circle in the middle for the house to stand on.

3 Mould brick shapes from self-hardening clay and build your house in a cylinder shape on the card, leaving a space for the entrance.

4 Paint the art straws yellow. Stick them all around the cone and trim them to make a thatched roof.

Mobile homes

Nomadic people move with their animals looking for land, food and water. Some carry their homes with them. Others build shelters and leave them behind when they move on.

The plains people of North America followed buffalo herds. They dragged a tent, called a tepee, along on a sledge.

Travelling around

In Europe, travellers used to move from place to place looking for work. They lived in decorated caravans pulled by a horse. Today, caravans are often used as mobile holiday homes. People travel from place to place with everything they need for sleeping, washing and cooking.

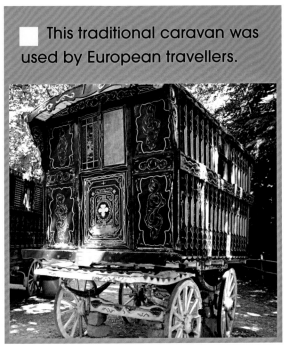

This traditional caravan was used by European travellers.

Make a model caravan

You will need:
- thin card • cardboard
- shoebox • scissors • hole punch • glue • paint and coloured pens • 2 straws
- poster putty or sticky tape

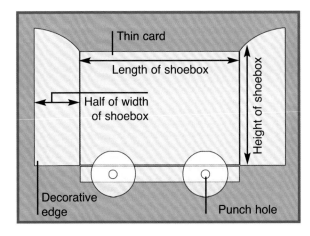

1 Cut the card, as shown above, to make one side of the caravan. Repeat for the other side. Punch holes for the wheel axles to go through. Stick the card to the shoebox to make the body of the caravan.

2 Cut a rectangle of card slightly bigger than the shoebox base and glue it onto the body for a curved roof. Cut four cardboard circles for the wheels and punch a hole in their centre.

3 Use bright paints (including gold and silver) or coloured pens to decorate the parts of your caravan. Use the picture on page 22 for ideas.

4 Push the straws through the axle holes and fix the wheels to the end of the straws with poster putty or sticky tape.

Eco-homes

Many new homes are **eco-homes**.
These are designed to be as kind to
the **environment** as possible. Older homes
can be adapted to be more eco-friendly.
A simple draught excluder, for example,
can stop heat escaping and save **energy**.

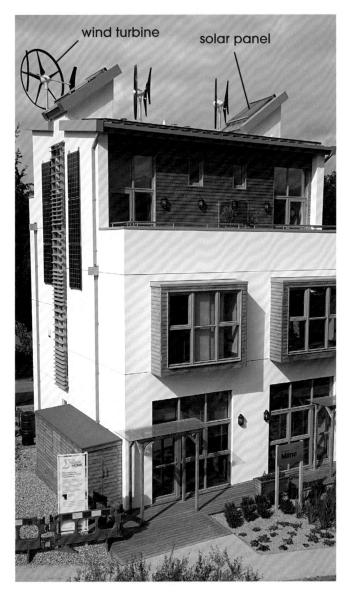

wind turbine

solar panel

Renewable energy

Eco-homes use renewable energy for heating and lighting. Renewable energy comes from sources such as sunlight, water and wind that will never run out. In most homes, **fossil fuels** are burned for energy. These fuels give out **carbon emissions** that harm the environment, and will eventually run out.

This eco-home has solar panels to heat water and wind turbines to generate electricity.

Make a difference

There are lots of things that can be done to make your home more environmentally friendly. **Double-glazing** the windows to keep out draughts, using **insulation** to keep in the heat, mending dripping taps and re-using bath water are just a few examples.

Loft insulation keeps a house warm and cosy. It helps to reduce heating bills, too!

How eco-friendly is your home?

1 Carry out a survey like the one shown below.

2 Tick the boxes and find out if your home is an eco-home.

3 Ask your family what changes you could make to improve things.

SAVE ENERGY	Double-glazing	Draught excluders	Stand-by off (TV, computer, etc.)
	✓	Make!	✓
SAVE WATER	**Mend dripping taps**	**Use shower instead of bath**	**Collect rainwater**
	✓	✓	Research!
PLANTS	**Wild area in garden**	**Green leafy plants**	**Window boxes**
	✓	✓	Make!

Unusual homes

All over the world, people live in unusual homes that probably look very different to your own home. In northern China, people carve homes out of the mountainside. They are easy and cheap to build!

These cave homes in China look very basic, but they have electricity and running water.

Ice and snow

Inuit people of the frozen Arctic traditionally build shelters called igloos. Blocks of packed snow provide shelter when the Inuit people are out on hunting and fishing trips.

This igloo is warm because snow keeps out the cold and keeps in the heat.

Reed islands

By Lake Titicaca in Peru, local people weave the reeds that grow around the lake into floating islands, shelters and boats. The women constantly repair and replace the reeds that rot in the water.

These shelters by Lake Titicaca are made using local reeds.

A day in the life...

Imagine what it would be like to live in any of the three homes described here.

Write about a day in your life, living in one of them.

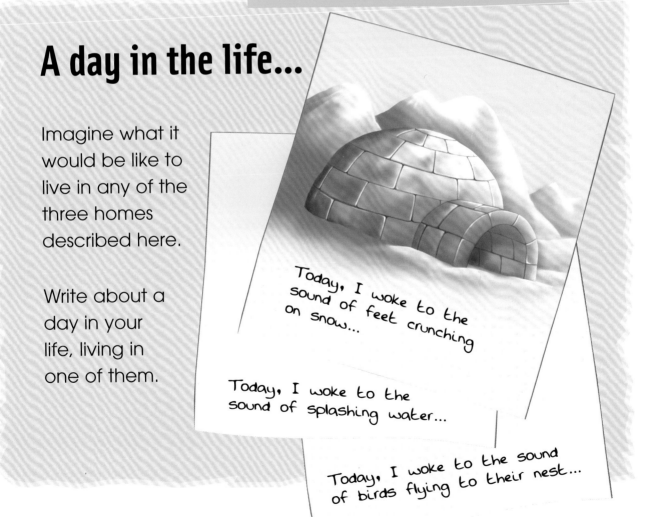

Today, I woke to the sound of feet crunching on snow...

Today, I woke to the sound of splashing water...

Today, I woke to the sound of birds flying to their nest...

Glossary

aerial view
An aerial view is a view looking down on the ground from above.

carbon emissions
Carbon emissions are gases containing carbon that are sent into the air when we burn fossil fuels such as coal, oil and gas.

climate
Climate is the kind of weather an area usually has. For example, the climate of a tropical rainforest is hot and wet all year round.

double-glazing
Double-glazing is when two panes of glass are fitted in a window frame to prevent heat from escaping.

eco-home
An eco-home is a home designed to be friendly to the planet. It may have solar panels to heat water and double-glazing to prevent heat loss, for example.

energy
Energy is the force that makes things move, heat up or change. Renewable energy comes from sources that can be replaced or that will never run out.

environment
Your environment is what is around where you live. Your environment might be the countryside, the seaside or a city.

fertile plain
A fertile plain is a large, flat area of land with rich soil suitable for growing crops.

flat
A flat is a home with its own front door inside a bigger building.

fossil fuels
Fossil fuels are coal, oil and natural gas. We burn them to make energy. Fossil fuels are formed from the remains of ancient plants and animals.

insulation

Insulation prevents heat escaping from homes. It can be a layer of material in the loft or foam pumped into the walls.

locality

A locality is a particular area. Your locality is the area that surrounds your home.

manufactured

Materials that are manufactured are made in a factory.

materials

Materials are what things are made of. For example, bricks, concrete and wood are all types of building materials.

new town

A new town is one that has been planned and built on an open piece of land with its own schools, shops and all the things people living there need.

nomadic

Nomadic people move from place to place grazing their animals or searching for work.

settlement

A settlement is a place where people decide to live and build permanent homes.

shelter

A shelter provides cover from the weather or protection from danger.

suburb

A suburb is an area of homes built on the edge of a town or a city.

trade

Trade is the buying and selling of goods.

traditions

Traditions are things that people have been doing for hundreds of years.

Index

caravan 22, 23
castle 19
city 6, 8, 9, 10
climate 12, 28

decoration 7
design 7, 12, 16, 17, 24
double-glazing 25, 28

eco-home 24, 25, 28

flat 6, 9, 10, 28
floor plan 17
fossil fuels 24, 28

garage 10

house 7, 9, 10, 12, 14, 17,
   18, 19, 20, 21, 22, 25

insulation 25, 29

landscape 12
locality 10, 11, 29

mansion 18, 19

materials 7, 12, 14,
   15, 18, 29

natural disaster 21
new town 9, 29
nomad 22, 29

renewable energy 24
roof 12, 14, 15
room 6, 16, 17, 21

settlement 8, 9, 29
shelter 8, 12, 16, 21, 22,
   26, 27, 29
suburb 10, 29

tourist attractions 18
town 6, 9, 20

villa 18
village 6, 11

walls 12, 14, 15, 18, 20
weather 7, 8, 12
windows 7, 12, 15, 25